Living and Working in Space

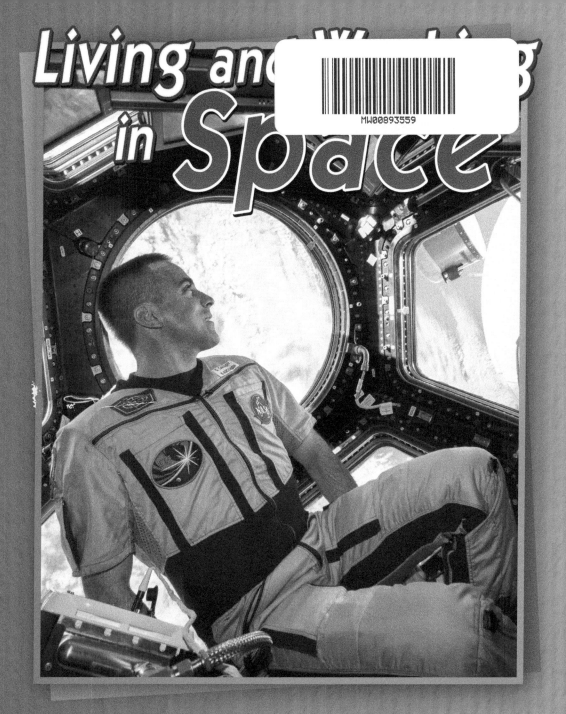

Nicole Sipe

✷ Smithsonian

Contributing Author

Allison Duarte

Consultants

Cathleen Lewis, Ph.D.
Curator of International Space Programs and Spacesuits
Smithsonian's National Air and Space Museum

Stephanie Anastasopoulos, M.Ed.
TOSA, STREAM Integration
Solana Beach School District

Publishing Credits

Rachelle Cracchiolo, M.S.Ed., *Publisher*
Conni Medina, M.A.Ed., *Managing Editor*
Diana Kenney, M.A.Ed., NBCT, *Content Director*
Véronique Bos, *Creative Director*
Robin Erickson, *Art Director*
Michelle Jovin, M.A., *Associate Editor*
Mindy Duits, *Senior Graphic Designer*
Smithsonian Science Education Center

Image Credits: front cover, pp.2–3, p.4, p.5 (all), p.6, p.7 (bottom), p.8, p.9, p.10, p.11 (all), p.12 (all), p.13 (all), p.14 (all), p.15, pp.16–17, p.16 (left), p.18, p.19, p.20, p.21 (top), p.22, p.23 (right), p.24 (all), p.25, p.26 (all), p.28, p.31, p.32 (all) NASA; back cover © Smithsonian; p.7 (top) European Space Agency; p.23 (left) Mark Williamson/Science Source; all other images from iStock and/or Shutterstock.

Library of Congress Cataloging-in-Publication Data

Names: Sipe, Nicole, author.
Title: Living and working in space / Nicole Sipe.
Description: Huntington Beach, CA : Teacher Created Materials, Inc., [2018] |
   Audience: Grades 4 to 6. | Includes index. |
Identifiers: LCCN 2018018116 (print) | LCCN 2018020662 (ebook) | ISBN
   9781493869527 (E-book) | ISBN 9781493867127 (pbk.)
Subjects: LCSH: Space stations--Juvenile literature. | Space
   environment--Juvenile literature. | Manned space flight--Juvenile
   literature. | Outer space--Exploration--Juvenile literature.
Classification: LCC TL797.15 (ebook) | LCC TL797.15 .S57 2018 (print) | DDC
   629.45--dc23
LC record available at https://lccn.loc.gov/2018018116

Teacher Created Materials

5301 Oceanus Drive
Huntington Beach, CA 92649-1030
www.tcmpub.com
ISBN 978-1-4938-6712-7

Table of Contents

Out of This World.. 4

The Right People for the Job 6

Home Sweet Space Station 10

A World of Work 14

Life in Space 18

Back on Earth and Beyond............................ 26

STEAM Challenge.. 28

Glossary 30

Index 31

Career Advice 32

Out of This World

Bzzzz! Your alarm goes off, singing its familiar wake-up song.
You open your eyes, yawn, and stretch your arms. It's time to start
another day.

You unstrap yourself from your sleeping bag and float over to the
bathroom. You grab your toothbrush, toothpaste, and a small bag of
water that sticks to the wall with Velcro®. You squeeze a bit of water from
the bag, but it slowly floats away from you.

"Not again!" you say. Fortunately, the rogue droplet doesn't get
very far. You catch it and watch as it seeps into the toothbrush bristles.
Success! Very carefully, you squeeze a bit of toothpaste onto your brush.
It stays put. Yes! Maybe, just maybe, you're starting to get the hang of
this microgravity thing.

Astronaut Clayton Anderson
watches a water droplet float.

Floating water (and floating everything) is just one of the many challenges astronauts face when they are living and working in space. When people are hundreds of kilometers from Earth, things work a little—sometimes a lot—differently!

The first astronauts in space only stayed for a short time to explore and do experiments. But now, scientists have the technology to send astronauts into space for over a year. Astronauts have everything they need to live and work in space.

Astronaut Samantha Cristoforetti drinks from a food packet.

Flight engineer Karen Nyberg demonstrates how fruit floats.

Astronauts are up to 5 centimeters (2 inches) taller in space because gravity does not put as much pressure on their spines.

The Right People for the Job

There is an old saying: "It's a tough job, but someone has to do it." This can apply to living and working in space. Living in space might sound like it would be a dream come true. Who wouldn't want to eat breakfast while floating 385 kilometers (240 miles) above Earth? But living in space is a lot of work. It can take up to two years of training and physical fitness before a person is ready for this important job.

The men and women who train to become astronauts are called astronaut candidates. Many people apply for this coveted, or desired, position. Very few are chosen. How few? The last time a call was put out for astronaut candidates, more than 18,000 people applied, but only 12 were chosen. Those are some tough odds!

The people who are chosen to be astronauts are the best of the best in their fields. They come from different career backgrounds. Some are teachers, engineers, scientists, or doctors before they become astronauts. However, to be chosen, they all need degrees in science, technology, engineering, or math.

NASA is the U.S. government agency that runs the country's space program. It stands for National Aeronautics and Space Administration.

An astronaut candidate climbs through a cave to adjust to the cramped living conditions in space.

Astronaut Reid Wiseman practices using tools before going to space.

Time to Train

Astronaut candidates train for space at NASA's Johnson Space Center in Houston, Texas. They take classes to learn everything they need to know for their time in space. They learn all about the space shuttles they will ride in and about the space station where they will live.

Candidates also take classes to learn Russian. This helps them communicate with their fellow astronauts from Russia. They also take classes to learn what to do during an emergency.

Candidates practice being in low gravity. But how can someone practice for this condition on Earth? The answer is by going underwater. Candidates take scuba lessons and do a lot of work in a deep tank called the Neutral **Buoyancy** Laboratory (NBL). Being in the tank feels a lot like being weightless in space. Underwater, your body feels light. People can move heavy objects easily. This is the same in space. Any jobs that need to be done in space are first practiced several times in the NBL.

Another way to get the body prepared for space is to spend time in a special airplane called the Weightless Wonder. This aircraft rises and falls as it flies. It allows people inside to feel weightless for 20 to 30 seconds at a time. Many people feel sick while in the aircraft, earning it the nickname "Vomit Comet." It can even make experienced astronauts lose their lunches!

Astronaut candidates experience weightlessness on the Weightless Wonder.

MATHEMATICS

parabola

One Sick Ride

The Weightless Wonder flies in a series of parabolas, or curves. This gives passengers the feeling of being weightless. To create each parabola, the plane makes a steep climb into the sky, and then dips down sharply, over and over again. As the plane drops, the passengers feel weightless. It is a similar feeling to what people experience when driving along a hilly road—only much more extreme!

Home Sweet Space Station

Training is done. The astronauts are as prepared as they can be. They blast off into space. But where are they going? They are heading to their home away from home—the International Space Station (ISS).

The ISS is like a giant, floating home and laboratory. It orbits 385 km (240 mi.) above Earth. It is where astronauts eat, sleep, work, and live while they are away.

On the ISS, there are areas to do work and a laboratory for experiments. It also has a living area where astronauts hang out when they are not working. The living area is about the size of a five-bedroom house. It has two bathrooms and a gym for exercising. The ISS might sound spacious, but it depends on how many people are on board. There can be up to 10 people on the ISS when a space shuttle is there.

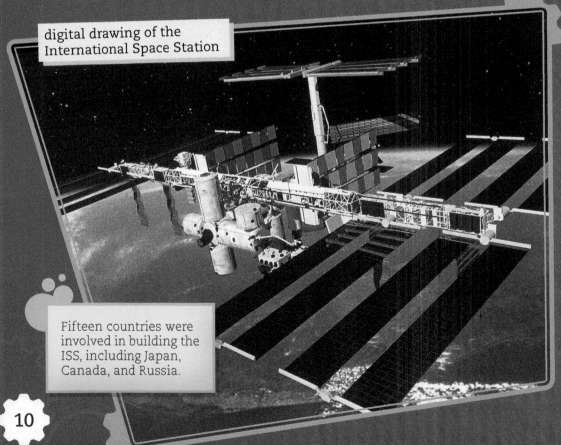

digital drawing of the International Space Station

Fifteen countries were involved in building the ISS, including Japan, Canada, and Russia.

One of astronauts' favorite features on the ISS is the Cupola. It is a dome with seven windows that lets viewers see all around them. This allows for some truly out-of-this-world views. Astronauts on the ISS get to see things in person that no one else sees in a lifetime. For instance, because the ISS makes one complete trip around Earth every 90 minutes, they get to see the sun rise and set 16 times per day!

Flight engineer Cady Coleman plays with her flutes inside the Cupola.

windows shown from the outside of the Cupola

People have been living on the ISS every day since 2000. Astronauts come and go from the space station. They usually stay for six months. Then, they head back to Earth.

Astronauts can live without a lot of things while they are in space. But they cannot live without one very important thing: **oxygen**. People need it to breathe. But space has very little breathable oxygen. Fortunately, the space station provides astronauts with the kind of air they need to live. Astronauts can also create oxygen by using water.

Some of the water used on the ISS is shipped from Earth. But a lot of water on the space station is **recycled**, cleaned, and used over and over again. This includes water that the astronauts drink and use to wash themselves. It even includes the tiny amounts of water that come from the astronauts' sweat, breath, and urine. Water can be either recycled and reused, or it can be used to create oxygen for the astronauts.

toilet

waste
management

urine
recycling

astronaut Jeffrey
Williams with a
urine recovery unit

clean
water
processing

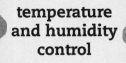

temperature and humidity control

astronaut Koichi Wakata with an oxygen generator

ISS Recycling Flow

oxygen created from water

crew uses oxygen

oxygen pumped into cabin

TECHNOLOGY

Breathing Easy

Recycling water to create oxygen is not a new method. This same technology has been used on submarines for many years. Submarines have machines that use **electrolysis** to break water into its molecules, or parts. The new gases are used for the crew to breathe. Submarines have more access to water than a space station, though. So they use ocean water to create breathable air for the crew.

A World of Work

Astronauts go to space for specific reasons. They are there to do research and experiments. The ISS was created to be a lab for astronauts. There, they can work in a setting that does not exist on Earth. Some things, such as microgravity, are unique to space. Things in space are also exposed to extreme cold and heat, as well as high levels of **radiation**. Astronauts can learn much while in space because of these conditions.

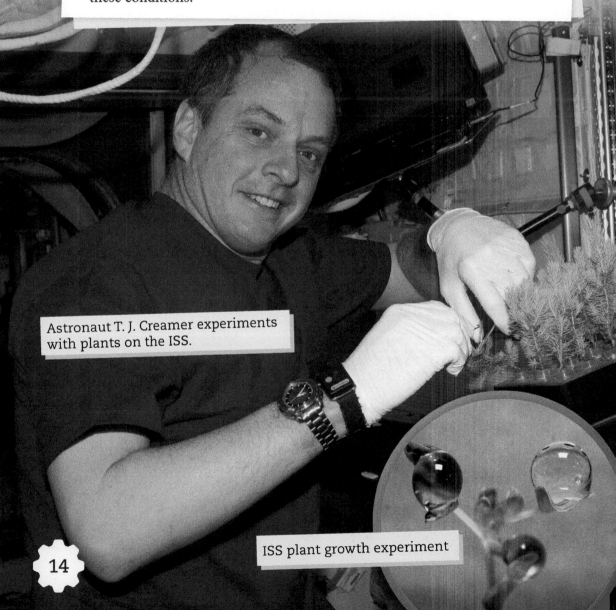

Astronaut T. J. Creamer experiments with plants on the ISS.

ISS plant growth experiment

So, what kinds of experiments take place in space? If you were on board the space station, you might see a lot of things happening. You might see astronauts working with fire to see how flames behave in space. You might see them studying plants, mice, or fish to see how being in lower gravity affects living things.

Astronauts also do experiments on themselves. They constantly monitor their health while they are in space. Scientists want to learn how living in space affects the human body. How does a body change in space? What are the risks of being there? The answers to these questions will help future astronauts and space missions.

Astronaut Karen Nyberg tests her eye health on the ISS.

The ISS is the third-brightest object in the night sky, after the moon.

Astronaut Roberto Vittori wears his landing suit.

ARTS

Space Suits

Astronauts wear colored space suits—usually orange—during takeoff and landing. They wear white suits when they go on spacewalks. The two colors are for practical purposes, not for fashion. The colored suit is for safety, as it is bright and stands out in an emergency. The white color reflects the strong heat of the sun and keeps astronauts from getting too hot.

Working in space also means taking care of the space station. The crew frequently checks the station's systems, air filters, and computer equipment. If something needs to be repaired, an astronaut on board must fix it.

Often, something on the outside of the space station will need repair or replacement. When this happens, astronauts go on **spacewalks** to fix it. But they cannot just open the door and step outside. There is no air in space! So astronauts put on space suits before leaving the station. Inside the space suits is pure oxygen, which they need to survive.

Astronauts must go through a series of steps before they go on spacewalks. They must put on space suits several hours before they plan to leave the space station. During this time, their suits fill with pure oxygen. As they breathe, they do some exercises and move their bodies. This gets rid of **nitrogen** in astronauts' bodies. If astronauts did not do these steps before walking into space, they might get painful gas bubbles. This condition is known as "the bends."

Spacewalks can take up to eight hours. When on spacewalks, astronauts cannot eat. There is no room in the suits for food! But if astronauts get thirsty, they can drink water through small straws from packs strapped to their chests.

Mission specialists David Wolf and Piers J. Sellers participate in a spacewalk outside the ISS.

Life in Space

What does a typical day in space look like? People might be surprised to learn that the daily lives of astronauts in space don't look much different from life on Earth—astronauts wake up, clean themselves, and get dressed. They eat, exercise, rest, work, and sleep. And then they do it all over again the next day. However, it's where and how they do it that's unusual.

Astronauts face incredible challenges while living in space. A lack of gravity, confined spaces, and being far from Earth all change the way they live and work.

Sleeping in Space

Astronauts sleep in sleeping bags attached to the walls of a small area called a crew cabin. The attached bags keep them from floating all over the space station while they rest. There is no up or down in space, so astronauts can sleep in any direction they want. To keep their arms and legs from floating in front of them while they sleep, they are secured to their sleeping bags.

There is also no morning or night in space. This makes sleeping in space very difficult because people are programmed to sleep when it's dark and be awake when it's light. Adjusting to sleeping on the space station can take astronauts several days or even weeks. Going to bed and waking up at the same time every day can help them adjust. Just like kids, astronauts have bedtimes!

Astronaut Koichi Wakata sleeps while strapped to a sleeping bag.

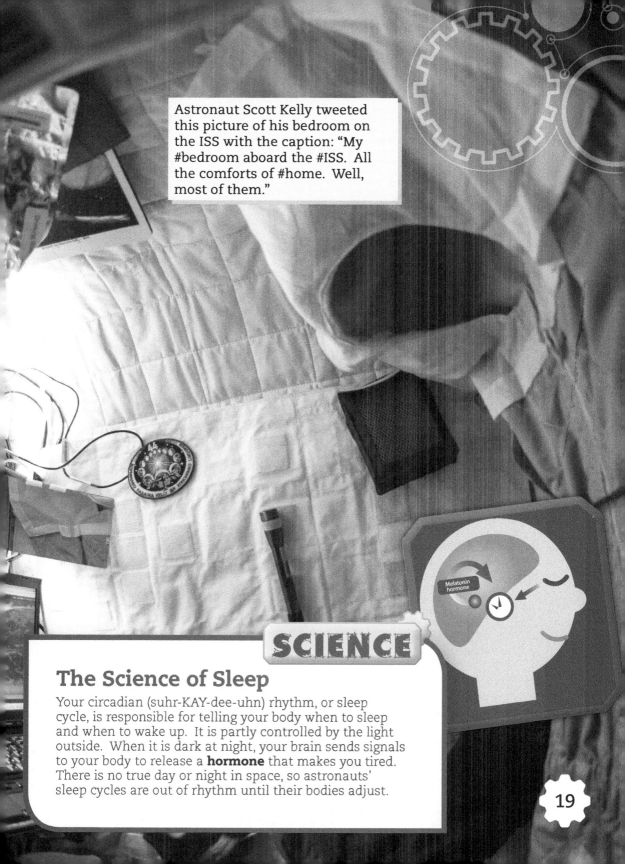

Astronaut Scott Kelly tweeted this picture of his bedroom on the ISS with the caption: "My #bedroom aboard the #ISS. All the comforts of #home. Well, most of them."

SCIENCE

The Science of Sleep

Your circadian (suhr-KAY-dee-uhn) rhythm, or sleep cycle, is responsible for telling your body when to sleep and when to wake up. It is partly controlled by the light outside. When it is dark at night, your brain sends signals to your body to release a **hormone** that makes you tired. There is no true day or night in space, so astronauts' sleep cycles are out of rhythm until their bodies adjust.

Melatonin hormone

Eating in Orbit

No one delivers pizza to space, so astronauts must bring their own food with them on their journeys. Scientists have created ways to package food that keep foods edible for many months. The food also has to be easy to eat in low gravity. In the early days of human spaceflight, food was not very appealing. There were gelatin-coated food cubes and applesauce in squeezable tubes. These were not exactly mouth-watering delights.

Fortunately, space food has improved. Astronauts in space eat many of the same things that people eat on Earth. The difference is that their food is vacuum-packed and then packaged on trays. Vacuum-packed food has had all the air sucked out before being sealed. With this method, astronauts can still enjoy meals such as tacos and shrimp cocktail. The only limitation to the foods they can eat is that they cannot drop crumbs. Those crumbs could clog up equipment!

Astronauts also have a wide-range of beverages available to them. They can choose from dehydrated pouches of lemonade, coffee, tea, and juice. They just add water through tubes to turn the beverages from powders into liquids.

Eating in microgravity is an adventure. To keep meals from floating away, astronauts attach food trays to their laps or strap them to walls.

These vacuum-packed packages of food and dehydrated beverages are used by astronauts.

Astronauts on the ISS prepare their lunches.

ENGINEERING

Eat Like an Astronaut

Freeze-drying food is another way to preserve it for use in space. To do so, food is frozen and then the ice is turned into a gas. This way, all the moisture is removed and the food won't spoil for a long time. Freeze-dried food isn't just used in space, either. You can find it in grocery stores, in the form of dried strawberries in breakfast cereal.

Keeping Clean

Good hygiene is important for everyone, even astronauts. Some would say it is *especially* important for astronauts, who are in close quarters all day, every day.

In space, staying clean is more challenging than it is on Earth due to the microgravity environment. Astronauts can't just turn on water at a sink and wash their hands. If they did, water drops would float all around them! While this would create a spectacular sight, it wouldn't get them clean. Astronauts must make a few adjustments when they are in space.

To clean their hair, astronauts use special shampoo that does not need to be rinsed out. To wash their bodies, they use wet towels. Any extra moisture from their "baths" gets sucked up by a hose. This water is recycled and used later as drinking water.

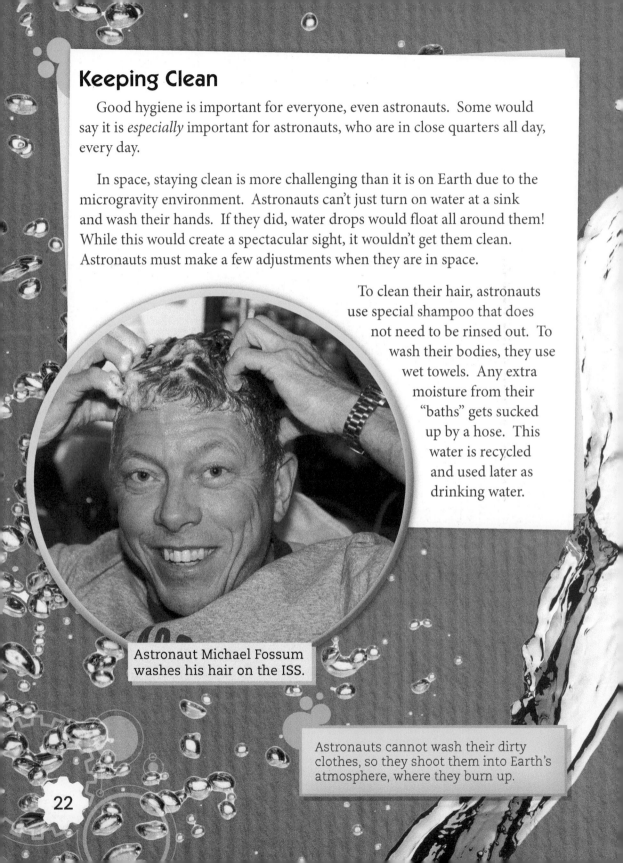

Astronaut Michael Fossum washes his hair on the ISS.

Astronauts cannot wash their dirty clothes, so they shoot them into Earth's atmosphere, where they burn up.

Brushing teeth in space is a lot like it is on Earth, except astronauts have special toothpaste that they can swallow when done. Astronauts can also shave in space. Any extra water from this task gets recycled as drinking water.

When astronauts have to use the bathroom, they first strap themselves over a small toilet to stay in place. The toilet has leg restraints to keep them from floating off while they are doing their business. The toilet acts like a vacuum and sucks waste into a tank. Urine is collected and recycled to be used later as—you guessed it—drinking water. Now, who's ready for a tasty beverage aboard the ISS?

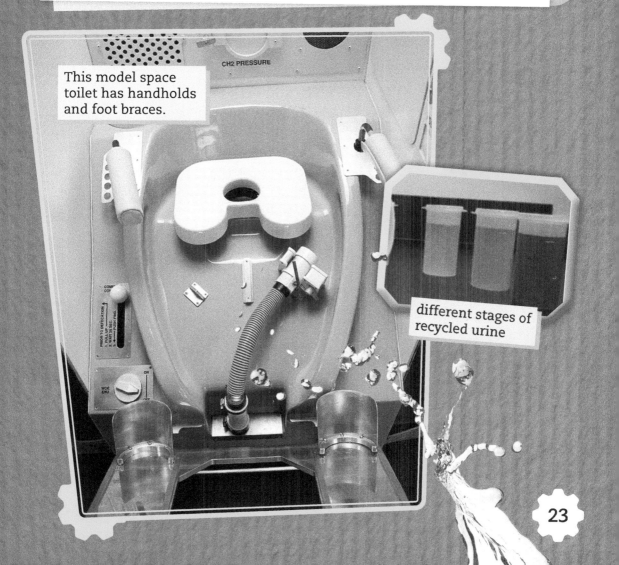

This model space toilet has handholds and foot braces.

different stages of recycled urine

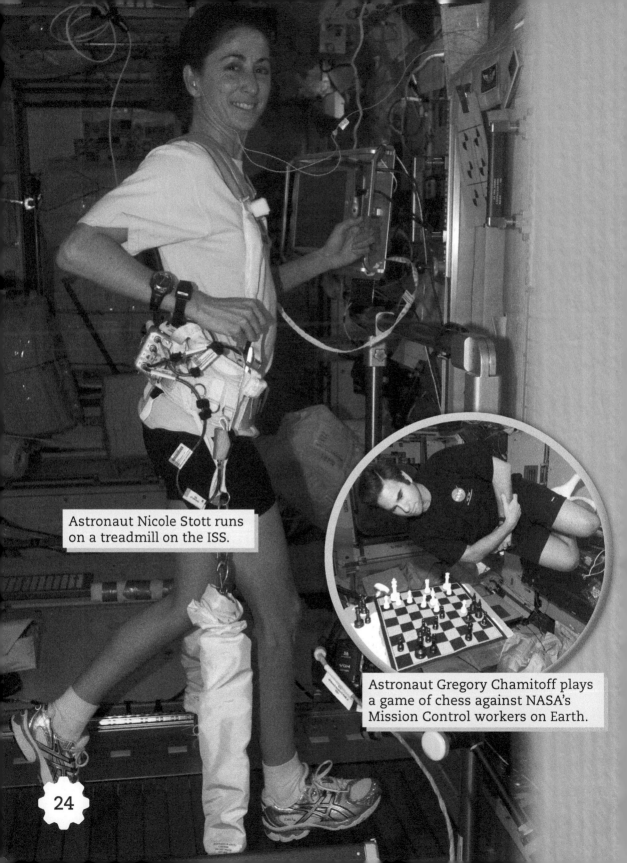

Astronaut Nicole Stott runs on a treadmill on the ISS.

Astronaut Gregory Chamitoff plays a game of chess against NASA's Mission Control workers on Earth.

Exercise Time

Astronauts exercise for at least two hours each day while they are in space. But it's not because they want to look tough when they come back to Earth. They are trying to prevent the loss of muscle and bone that happens to bodies in space. Space travel and microgravity are hard on a person's body. Exercising keeps muscles and bones strong.

A small gym area is on the space station. It has a treadmill, a stationary bike, and a weight machine. Astronauts strap themselves to the equipment when they work out so they don't float away. As they exercise, doctors on Earth monitor them to make sure they stay healthy.

Downtime

Astronauts work hard, but they also need time to relax. Free time is built into their schedules every day. They also get weekends off. During free time, astronauts read books, watch movies, play board games, or use computers to talk to family on Earth.

One of the most popular pastimes is just sitting and looking out the window. Astronauts get a front row seat to the most spectacular views of Earth and space. Very few people get to see the sights they do!

Astronauts Anton Shkaplerov and Daniel Burbank play music in their free time.

The lack of gravity in space pulls blood to the head and chest. This makes astronauts' faces look puffy and gives them headaches.

Back on Earth and Beyond

It is great to live and work in space, but sometimes there's no place like home. Astronauts typically spend six months in space at one time. When they come back to Earth, they must get used to certain things—namely gravity. They have been weightless for months, so they must readjust to the pressure that gravity places on their bodies. It takes them a while to relearn how to walk, stand, and hold objects.

Astronauts make big sacrifices when they go into space. They are away from family for a long time. They live in cramped quarters with many other people. And they risk their lives every day. But astronauts willingly make these sacrifices to explore new frontiers in space.

The people who live and work aboard the ISS are paving the way for future space explorations. NASA plans to send humans even deeper into space. NASA could send the first humans to an asteroid by 2025. By 2030, the first people might be landing on Mars. The things scientists learn now from astronauts who live and work in space are helping to make this dream a reality.

The *Soyuz TMA-21* spacecraft safely returns to Earth in 2011.

NASA Commander Randy Bresnik celebrates returning to Earth.

This graphic shows what space travel might look like in the future.

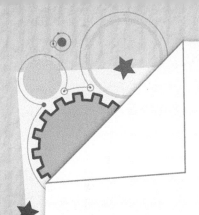

STEAM CHALLENGE

Define the Problem

Conditions in space are much different from life on Earth! Scientists and engineers have developed tools and equipment to help astronauts live and work in space. Some experiments involve astronauts collecting specimens during spacewalks. Your task is to design and build a specialized tool that improves the daily lives of astronauts in microgravity.

Constraints: Your tool must be no longer than 30 cm (12 in.).

Criteria: Test your design by having a friend use it successfully.

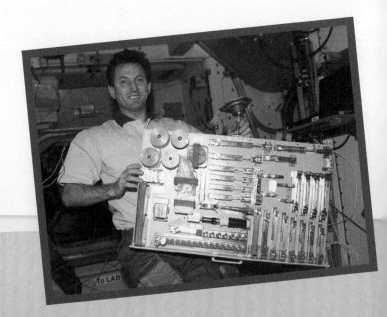

Research and Brainstorm

How are conditions in space different from conditions on Earth? What are some examples of tools and equipment that help astronauts adapt to life in space?

Design and Build

Sketch a design of your tool. What purpose will each part serve? What materials will work best? Build the model.

Test and Improve

Demonstrate how your tool works. How might you change your tool to make it work better? Modify your design and try again.

Reflect and Share

What other materials can you use to build this new tool? How will your tool make astronauts' lives easier in space? What other types of tools might be useful to astronauts who live and work in space?

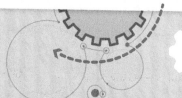

Glossary

asteroid—a small, rocky object that orbits the sun

buoyancy—the ability to float in water or air

candidates—people who are being considered for a job

confined—very small

coveted—greatly wished for

dehydrated—having all water removed

edible—able to be eaten

electrolysis—the process of separating a liquid into its different chemical parts by passing an electric current through the liquid

gelatin—a clear, tasteless protein

hormone—a natural substance produced by the body, which influences how the body grows or develops

microgravity—very weak gravity

nitrogen—a gas that makes up a large part of the air on Earth

oxygen—a gas that is necessary for life

programmed—made to behave a certain way

radiation—a form of dangerous and powerful energy that is given off by radioactive substances and nuclear reactions

recycled—processed in order to reuse

rogue—used to describe something that is different from others

spacewalks—time spent in space outside spacecraft

spacious—having a large amount of space or room

Index

astronaut candidates, 6–9

Canada, 10

circadian rhythm, 19

Houston, Texas, 8

hygiene, 22

International Space Station (ISS),
    10–17, 19, 21–24

Japan, 10

Johnson Space Center, 8

Mars, 26

microgravity, 4, 14, 20, 22, 25

moon, 16

National Aeronautics and Space
    Administration (NASA), 6–8,
    24, 26

Neutral Buoyancy Laboratory
    (NBL), 8

Russia, 8, 10

space suits, 16–17

spacewalks, 16–17

submarines, 13

"the bends," 17

Velcro, 4

Weightless Wonder, 8–9

CAREER ADVICE
from Smithsonian

Do you want to work in the space industry?
Here are some tips to get you started.

"Before becoming an educator at the Air and Space Museum, I was a teacher. I studied STEAM in school, but I also studied English and communications. Those subjects helped me teach people about what life is like in space!" —*Marty Kelsey, Host of STEM in 30*

"Study as many different topics as you can. I study STEAM subjects, but I also learn as much as I can about topics. I read about astronomy, physics, English, and European history to do my job. Space history is about passion and enthusiasm. Find what you love to study and you can do anything you put your mind and heart to!" —*Peter L. Jakab, Chief Curator*